# WAZWAAN

# WAZWAAN
## *Traditional Kashmiri Cuisine*

❋

*Khan Mohammed Sharief Waza*

❋

*Khan Mohammed Shafi Waza*

❋

*Khan Mohammed Rafiq Waza*

❋

*Photographs: Dheeraj Paul*

*Rocky Mohan*
.cookery club.
**Roli Books**

*Bismillah Irahman Irahim*

To our father
Khan Abdul Ahad Waza who
popularised *wazwaan* worldwide

ISBN: 81-7436-171-5

Text: Rocky Mohan
Photographs: Dheeraj Paul

© **Roli & Janssen BV 2001**
Published in India by Roli Books
in arrangement with Roli & Janssen BV
M-75 Greater Kailash, II (Market)
New Delhi 110 048, India.
Phone: 6442271, 6462782; Fax: 6467185
E-mail: roli@vsnl.com; Website: rolibooks.com

Designed at Roli CAD Centre

Printed and bound at Singapore

# Contents

# Introduction

*Agar firdaus bar ruhe zamin ast*
*Hamin asto, hamin asto, hamin asto.*

If there be a paradise on earth; it is this, it is this, it is this – these famous words have been attributed to the Mughal Emperor Jahangir, who was enraptured by the enthralling beauty of Kashmir. The chronology of the kings of the valley, *Raj Tarangini*, written by Kalhana, eulogises Kashmir and says it is 'imbued with the beauty of the Goddess Parvati; and its owner is Lord Shiva himself.' Bernier, who was the first European to visit Kashmir, as early as 1665, called it 'a kingdom of unsurpassed beauty.' Francis Younghusband, another great admirer, in his well-known book on Kashmir, writes: 'When the clouds roll by, the haze lifts and a real Kashmir spring or autumn discloses itself, the heart of even the hardest visitor melts and he becomes a Bernier himself!'

Kashmir has always been a Utopia for poets, artists, dreamers, and for less gifted, ordinary mortals as well. Surrounded by three Himalayan ranges, the Karakoram, the Zanaskar and the Pir Panjal, majestic with snow-covered peaks, its idyllic panoramic splendour draws people the world over to it. Every season brings with it new vistas – spring, when the air is heady with the fragrance of a million flowers that blossom on trees, shrubs and creepers; summer and autumn, with their vivid colours and mellow fruitfulness; and winter, magically painting the landscape in pristine white.

According to legend, the valley of Kashmir was once a large lake, and in it lived a demon who was killed after the lake was drained, with the help of Brahma's grandson, Kashyap, and the Goddess Parvati. Parvati is supposed to have killed the demon by dropping a mountain on him. This legendary mountain is believed to be *Takht-i-Sulaiman* or Shankaracharya, which forms the famous backdrop to the city of Srinagar.

History and myth, language and literature, art and architecture, culture and tradition are distinctive features emphasising the individuality of the people of Kashmir, but they are also closely intertwined with and are an integral part of the Indian subcontinent. It was in this valley that Buddhism reached the zenith of its glory, Hinduism extended its frontiers into Shaivism and Shaktism, and Islam acquired a new meaning in the practice of Sufism. Kashmir can claim the distinction of being the melting pot of a multifaceted, unique and harmonious cultural blend. Its versatile cultural forms, fairs and festivals, rites and rituals, seers and sagas, cuisine and language, with its roots embedded in antiquity, speak of unity in diversity and unparalleled cultural cohesion – called *kashmiriyat*.

The scenic beauty of Kashmir is only rivalled by its cuisine, which offers an infinite and sumptuous variety of both vegetarian and non-vegetarian delicacies – perhaps nowhere else in India can one find food as unique and elaborate, which pampers the taste buds of the most fastidious of gourmets. It is born of the marriage of the rich, cultural heritage of the land and diverse influences – Hindu, Buddhist, Afghan, Mughal, Sikh and British. Kashmiri cuisine is of two distinct types – *wazwaan* is the food of the Muslims, and the Pandits have their traditional *butta*. They share a love for lamb; wood fire to cook their mouth-watering delicacies, of which many are common to both. What is very evident is that both have been greatly influenced by the Mughlai style of cooking. The main difference is that the Pandits do not use onions and garlic, while Muslims utilise these in good measure.

According to local belief, when Timur invaded India in the 15th century, in his wake came 1700 skilled woodcarvers, weavers, calligraphers, architects and cooks from Samarkand, who settled in the valley of Kashmir. The descendants of these cooks, the *wazas*, are the master chefs of Kashmir. *Waan* in Kashmiri means 'shop'. A *wazwaan* is literally, therefore, a cook shop or restaurant.

In practice, however, the *wazwaan* is an elaborate and sumptuous ritual: a feast served to an honoured guest. This lavish hospitality must in turn be fully appreciated by the guest, for it is not just a meal but a ceremony. Hours of cooking and days of planning go into the preparation and serving of a *wazwaan*. Normally restricted to special occasions and celebrations at home, the *wazwaan* experience begins with table settings laid out for groups of four, who are seated on the floor and share the meal served on a large metal plate called a *trami*. First there is the ritual washing of hands in a basin called a *tash-t-nari*, which is taken around by attendants, and the diners wash their hands with warm water. Then the *tramis* arrive, each heaped with rice, accompanied by four *seekh kababs*, four pieces of *methi maaz*, one *tabakh maaz*, one *safed murg*, one *zafrani murg* – this is the first course. Yoghurt and chutney are served separately in small earthen pots. Choice dishes are served, fragrant with herbs, one after the other, each made with fresh, local produce. The animals are slaughtered ceremonially and expertly according to Muslim custom, and the *waza* (chief cook) personally supervises the preparation of each dish that emerges from his kitchen – every ingredient for the meal is handpicked, and much toil and effort ensures that each dish is a culinary masterpiece. The *wazas'* recipes are secret, locked away in their heads, passed on from generation to generation.

The ultimate formal grand banquet in Kashmir is the royal *wazwaan*. Of its 36 courses, between 15 and 30 are meat preparations, cooked all night by the *vasta waza* (master chef) and his retinue of *wazas*. Seven dishes must be a part of the meal on these occasions – *tabakh maaz*, *rista*, *rogan josh*, *dhaniwal korma*, *aab gosh*, *marchwagan korma* and *ghushtaba*. A variety of kebabs and vegetable preparations are also served. This veritable feast is rounded off with *ghushtaba*, a delicious *wazwaan* speciality made of pounded mutton balls in a yoghurt-based gravy.

*Firin* (saffron-flavoured semolina garnished with dry fruits) is the dessert, followed by *kahwah*, the green tea flavoured with saffron, cardamoms and almonds, and the *wazwaan* is over – a repast fit for a king and a never-to-be-forgotten experience of royal Kashmiri hospitality.

# Special Kashmiri Culinary Ingredients

1.  **Cashew nuts** (*kaju*): Cashew nuts spoil easily. Avoid buying shrivelled nuts that smell rancid. Dry-roasted cashew nuts contain less fat than any other kind of nut, and they are an excellent source of minerals and folic acid.

2.  **Walnuts** (*akhrot / doon*): Walnuts must be used or eaten quickly after being shelled as they deteriorate quickly in heat, humidity and direct sunlight.

3.  **Red kidney beans** (*rajmah / razmah*): These beans are the main ingredient for the well-known Kashmiri dish, *razmah*.

4.  **Shallots** (*praan*): Choose shallots that are firm and dry skinned. Avoid sprouted, soft or blemished ones. Shallots are more commonly used as a condiment than as a vegetable and lend a touch of refinement to the dish. Once cooked they are more easily digestible than onions.

5.  ***Zirish*** are berries indigenous to Kashmir.

6.  **Red chilli pepper** (*lal mirch / marchwagan*): Red chilli pepper is a fleshy berry with seeds in its inner cavity. There are some 100 known varieties that are grown. Be cautious when adding it to a dish, and do not exceed the recommended measure in the recipe.

7.  **Almonds** (*badam*): Almonds can be used to complement all kinds of food because of their mild flavour. They are added to both sweet and savoury dishes.

8.  **Tamarind** (*imli / tamar*): The word tamarind is derived from the Arabic word *tamar Hindi*, which means 'date of India'. The bitter-sweet, highly acidic pulp of the tamarind is used to flavour foods, and it is a good source of iron, potassium and magnesium.

9.  **Dried plums** (*alubukhara / alubukhar*): Dried plums, like all dried fruits, are fruits from which a major part of the water content has been removed.

10. **Pistachios** (*pista*): A relative of the cashew nut, pistachio nuts are often sold roasted and salted in their shells. They are very rich in minerals, vitamins and dietary fibre.

# *Kashmiri Spices and Condiments*

1. **Dry mint leaves** (*pudina / pudn*): Mint leaves are an aromatic herb which have been used from ancient times.
2. **Cloves** (*laung / roung*): Cloves are the dried flower buds of an evergreen plant. Clove oil contains phenol, which is a good antiseptic and helps in preserving food.
3. **Turmeric** (*haldi / lader*): Turmeric is a rhizome belonging to the the ginger family and is orange-yellow in colour.
4. **Black cardamoms** (*bari elaichi / budaul*): A variety of cardamom which has a heavier flavour than the green cardamoms.
5. **Saffron** (*zafran / kong*): The world's most expensive spice, saffron, must be soaked in either warm milk or water, and added to a dish after it is cooked.
6. **Coriander** (*dhaniya / dhaniwal*): Coriander powder is a spice which is indispensible spice in Indian cuisine, and fresh coriander leaves are used to garnish dishes. Coriander has a strong and pungent odour.
7. **Fennel powder** (*saunf / badayna*): Fennel powder is a common ingredient used to flavour stocks, sauces, pickles and curries.
8. **Cinnamon** (*dalchini*): Most Indian food is cooked with cassia bark, which is a good substitute for real cinnamon. However, it has a stronger flavour than that of cinnamon, which is more delicately flavoured.
9. **Black cardamoms seeds** (*bari elaichi dana / budaul dana*)
10. **Cumin seeds** (*jeera / zur*): There are two varieties of cumin seeds: white and black. The white variety is the more common one, while the black one is more aromatic and peppery.
11. **Dry fenugreek leaves** (*kasoori methi / meeth*)
12. **Dry cockscomb flower** (*mawal*): This is indigenous to Kashmiri cuisine.
13. **Dry ginger powder** (*sonth / shount*): This is made by drying fresh ginger root and then grinding it to a powder.
14. **Fennel seeds** (*saunf / badayna*)
15. **Green cardamoms** (*choti elaichi / eaul*): These are aromatic with a delicate flavour. The flavour is strongest when the seeds are ground to a powder.
16. **Red chilli powder** (*lal mirch / marchwagan*): There are at least 20 known varieties of chilli powders. Chillies range in colour from white and yellow to saffron and red.

# Basic Recipes

## Dry Cockscomb Flower Extract

Heat $1\frac{1}{2}$ cups dry cockscomb flowers with $1\frac{1}{2}$ cups water in a pan for 1-2 minutes. Cool and then strain through a fine muslin cloth. Collect the extract in a bowl. Use as required.

## Cooked Yoghurt

Whisk 2 cups yoghurt (*dahi*) until very smooth. Add $\frac{1}{2}$ cup water and whisk again to blend well. Pour this mixture into a round-bottomed pan and put it on high heat. Stir constantly till the mixture comes to the boil. Then reduce the heat to low, stirring occasionally, until the mixture is reduced to half its original quantity, and its colour has changed to off-white. Use this cooked yoghurt as specified in the recipes.

## Garlic Water

Mince $1\frac{1}{2}$ tbsp garlic (*lasan*) and mix it with $\frac{1}{4}$ cup water. Let it stand for 5 minutes. Rub the mixture, with your hands, through a fine muslin cloth, and collect the extract. Use as required.

## *Ghushtaba* and *Rista*

Take 500 gm fresh, boneless meat from the leg of lamb (with fat removed) and cut into 1"x 2" cubes; 4 tbsp fat or unsalted butter; $\frac{1}{4}$ tsp green cardamom (*choti elaichi*) powder and $\frac{3}{4}$ tbsp salt.

First, pound the meat on a smooth stone with a wooden mallet. While pounding, remove any white tough fibre that may appear. Keep pounding until the meat changes colour.

When the meat has lightened in colour, add the fat or unsalted butter and the green cardamom powder. Continue to pound with the mallet, turning it over with one hand, until the meat is very light in colour, soft and has a paste-like texture. Add the salt and pound until it is well mixed.

With hands wet in chilled water, make balls with the meat paste, and keep aside for use either for *ghushtaba* or *rista*.

| | |
|---|---|
| Weight per ball of *ghushtaba* : | 100 gm each |
| Weight per ball of *rista* : | 75 gm each |
| Weight per ball of *palak rista* : | 10 gm each |

## Ver Paste

Pound together 250 gm garlic (*lasan*) and 250 gm shallots (*praan*) to a coarse paste. Dry roast 1 kg Kashmiri red chilli powder, 50 gm black cardamoms (*bari elaichi*); 1 tbsp black cumin seeds (*shah jeera*); 1 tbsp green coriander (*choti elaichi*) seeds; 1 tbsp cinnamon (*dalchini*) powder; 1 tbsp dry ginger powder (*sonth*), separately. Then grind to a fine powder.

Mix the garlic and shallot paste with this powder. Shape them into cakes and make a hole in the centre big enough to pass a thin rope through it so that the cakes can be strung together and kept for use later. Dry the cakes in the sun until they have no moisture left.

# Seekh Kabab

*Skewered lamb kebabs*

### Ingredients

| | | | |
|---|---|---|---|
| 1 kg | hind leg of lamb, without fat, boneless | ¾ tsp / 1½ gm | black cumin seeds (*shah jeera*) |
| 4 tsp / 8 gm | Kashmiri red chilli powder | 1¼ tsp / 1½ gm | saffron (*zafran*), ground to a powder |
| 3 tsp / 12 gm | salt | 1 tbsp / 4 gm | green coriander (*hara dhaniya*), chopped |
| 1 tsp / 2 gm | black cardamom (*bari elaichi*) seeds, powdered | 1 tsp / 2 gm | dry mint (*pudina*) leaves |
| 2 | eggs, lightly beaten | | |

### Method

1. Chop the meat coarsely with a meat chopper on a hard wooden board. While chopping, add the red chilli powder and salt. Continue to chop the meat, turning it over with hands dipped in ice-cold water until the red chillies and salt are well mixed. Collect the chopped meat in a dish and refrigerate in the freezer for 1 hour.

2. Remove the chopped meat from the freezer and mix well. Then pass it through a mincing machine twice. Add the black cardamom powder, eggs, black cumin seeds, saffron, green coriander and dry mint leaves. Blend well.

3. Divide the mixture into 8 equal-sized portions and keep aside on a greased tray. Moisten hands with ice-cold water and mould one portion around a skewer, pressing and shaping it to the size of a 6"-long sausage. Moisten hands again and smoothen the surface of the kebab.

4. Roast it over a low charcoal fire, turning the skewer frequently until the kebab is reddish brown all over. Repeat the procedure till all the kebabs are done.

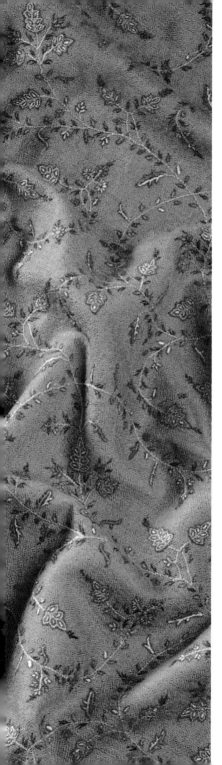

# Shami Kabab

*Minced lamb patties*

## Ingredients

| | | | |
|---|---|---|---|
| 500 gm | hind leg of lamb, boneless, cut into cubes | 1½ tsp / 3 gm | turmeric (*haldi*) powder |
| 10 cups / 2 lt | water | 1½ tsp / 3 gm | dry ginger powder (*sonth*) |
| ¾ cup / 120 gm | Bengal gram (*chana dal*) | 4 pieces | ginger (*adrak*), cut into 1" x 1" size |
| 6 | black cardamoms (*bari elaichi*) | 1 tbsp / 18 gm | garlic (*lasan*) paste |
| 12 | green cardamoms (*choti elaichi*) | 5 | green chillies, chopped |
| 4 | cinnamon (*dalchini*) sticks, 1" each | 1 tsp / 2 gm | black cumin seeds (*shah jeera*) |
| 2 tsp / 4 gm | Kashmiri red chilli powder | 1 tbsp / 4 gm | green coriander (*hara dhaniya*), chopped |
| Salt to taste | | Refined oil for frying | |

## Method

1. In a pan, add the meat, water, Bengal gram, black and green cardamoms, cinnamon sticks, red chilli powder, salt, turmeric powder, dry ginger powder, ginger and garlic paste. Bring the mixture to the boil. Reduce the heat and continue to cook it until all the water has evaporated and the meat is tender.
2. Remove the pan from the heat and keep aside to cool. Discard the whole spices. Pass the meat twice through a mincing machine, adding the green chillies, black cumin seeds and green coriander.
3. Divide the mixture equally into lemon-sized portions and shape each into a patty. Heat the refined oil in a pan; deep-fry the patties until golden brown. Remove and drain the excess oil on kitchen towels.

# Tabakh Maaz

*Delicious ribs – a Kashmiri delicacy*

## Ingredients

| | | | |
|---|---|---|---|
| 1 kg | rib cage (only the membranous part of the ribs, not the chop), unseparated | 2 tsp / 8 gm | salt |
| | | 2 tsp / 4 gm | dry ginger powder (*sonth*) |
| | | 8 | cloves (*laung*) |
| 27½ cups / 5½ lt | water | 8 | black cardamoms (*bari elaichi*) |
| 4½ tsp / 27 gm | garlic (*lasan*), ground | | |
| 3½ tsp / 14 gm | salt | 3½ tsp / 7 gm | turmeric (*haldi*) powder |
| 12½ cups / 2½ lt | water, cold | 2½ cups / 475 gm | pure (*desi*) ghee |

## Method

1. Bring the water to the boil; add the ribs. Continue to boil, removing the scum that rises to the surface. Repeat until the water is clear. Boil covered till the ribs are half done.

2. Add the garlic and mix well. Continue to boil for another 10 minutes. Add the salt and boil covered, continuously, until the membrane between the ribs can be pierced with the thumb. Remove the pan from the heat and drain the water. Cool the ribs and then immerse in a pan of cold water. Wash thoroughly, and then keep them aside. Do not discard this water.

3. Chop the ribs with a heavy, sharp knife into 8 equal rectangular pieces.

4. Boil the water in which the ribs were washed. Add the chopped ribs, salt, dry ginger powder, cloves, black cardamoms and turmeric powder. Mix well. Let it boil until the bones can be extracted from the membrane easily. Remove the pan from the heat and take out the ribs with a slotted spoon. Keep aside. Discard the water.

5. Arrange the ribs in a large frying pan, so that they do not overlap. Pour the pure ghee over them. Fry until they are reddish brown all over. Turn occasionally. Drain out the pure ghee before serving.

# Marchwagan Korma

*Red hot meat curry*

## Ingredients

| | | | |
|---|---|---|---|
| 1 kg | meat, cut into pieces | 4 tsp / 8 gm | turmeric (*haldi*) powder |
| 12½ cups / 2½ lt | water | 5 | cinnamon (*dalchini*) sticks, |
| 1 cup / 190 gm | pure (*desi*) ghee | | 2" each |
| Salt to taste | | 2 tsp / 4 gm | dry ginger powder (*sonth*) |
| 1 tbsp / 18 gm | garlic (*lasan*), ground | 1½ cups / 300 ml | dry cockscomb (*mawal*) |
| 10 | green cardamoms (*choti* | | flowers, heated with 1½ |
| | *elaichi*) | | cups water, extract |
| 5 | cloves (*laung*) | | (see p. 17) |
| 1½ cups | Kashmiri red chilli powder, | 1 tsp / 2 gm | black cumin seeds (*shah* |
| | dissolved in 10 cups water | | *jeera*) |
| 4 | black cardamoms (*bari* | 1 tsp / 2 gm | dry mint (*pudina*) leaves, |
| | *elaichi*) | | crushed |

## Method

1. Bring the water to the boil in a pan; add the meat. Mix well and then bring the water to the boil again. Remove the pan from the heat and drain the water. When the meat is cool, wash under cold running water. Keep aside.

2. In a pan, add the blanched meat, pure ghee, salt, garlic, green cardamoms and cloves. Mix well. Fry until the meat is light brown in colour.

3. Add the red chilli water, black cardamoms, turmeric powder, cinnamon sticks and dry ginger powder. Stir and bring the mixture to the boil. Lower the heat, cover the pan and cook until the meat is tender. Add some water, if necessary. Stir occasionally.

4. Add the cockscomb flower extract, black cumin seeds and dry mint leaves. Mix well and let the mixture simmer for 3-4 minutes.

# Alubukhar Korma

*Tangy lamb cooked with dried plums*

## Ingredients

| | | | |
|---|---|---|---|
| 1 kg | hind leg of lamb, cut into pieces | | powder, dissolved in ½ cup water |
| 12½ cups / 2½ lt | water | 4 | cinnamon (*dalchini*) sticks, 2" each |
| 1 cup / 190 gm | pure (*desi*)ghee | | |
| 8 | green cardamoms (*choti elaichi*) | 150 gm | tamarind (*imli*), boiled in 2 cups water for 10 minutes, strained |
| 4 | cloves (*laung*) | | |
| Salt to taste | | 2 tsp / 4 gm | turmeric (*haldi*) powder |
| ¼ cup / 50 ml | garlic (*lasan*) water (see p.17) | | |
| 3 tsp / 6 gm | Kashmiri red chilli | 1 cup | dried plums (*alu bukhara*) |

## Method

1. Boil the water in a deep pan; add the meat and bring the water to the boil again. Boil for 2 minutes. Remove from the heat and drain the water. Wash the meat in cold water and keep aside.

2. Put the meat in a pan and add the pure ghee, green cardamoms, cloves, salt, garlic water, red chilli water and cinnamon sticks. Cook, stirring continuously, until the ghee separates from the masala.

3. Add just enough water so that when the meat is tender very little water remains. Cook covered till the meat is done. Add the tamarind extract, turmeric powder and dried plums. Mix well, and simmer for 5-7 minutes, or till the plums are soft.

# Badam Korma

*Tender mutton in creamy almond*

### Ingredients

| | | | |
|---|---|---|---|
| 1 kg | hind leg of lamb, cut into 1½" x 1½" x 1½" cubes | 5 | cloves (*laung*) |
| 10 cups / 2 lt | water | + | cinnamon (*dalchini*) sticks, 1" each |
| 1 cup / 190 gm | pure (*desi*) ghee | ½ cup | almonds (*badam*), blanched, peeled, made into a fine, smooth paste with ½ cup milk |
| 10 | green cardamoms (*choti elaichi*) | | |
| Salt to taste | | | |
| ½ cup / 100 ml | garlic (*lasan*) water (see p. 17) | ½ cup / 100 ml | full cream |

(see p. 17)

### Method

1. Boil the water, add the meat and blanch for 1-2 minutes. Drain the water and wash meat in cold water. Keep aside.
2. In a pan, add the meat, ghee, green cardamoms, salt, garlic water, cloves, and cinnamon sticks. Mix well and bring the mixture to the boil, stirring continuously. Fry until the meat changes colour to a very light brown. Add enough water so that when the meat is tender very little water remains .
3. When the meat is soft, remove the pan from the heat and cool. Add the almond paste. Pour in the cream and mix well. Return the pan to very low heat and simmer the mixture, stirring all the time. Heat through.

Lamb

# Dhaniwal Korma

*Lamb in a yoghurt-based gravy garnished with green coriander*

## Ingredients

| | | | |
|---|---|---|---|
| 1 kg | leg of lamb, cut into pieces | 1 cup / 200 ml | cooked yoghurt (see p. 17) |
| 12½ cups / 2½ lt | water | ½ tsp / 1 gm | turmeric (*haldi*) powder |
| 1 cup / 190 gm | pure (*desi*) ghee | | |
| ⅓ cup / 80 ml | onion, puréed | 1½ tsp / 2 gm | coriander (*dhaniya*) powder |
| 1 tsp / 6 gm | garlic (*lasan*), ground | ¼ tsp | black pepper (*kali mirch*) powder |
| 4 | cloves (*laung*) | | |
| 8 | green cardamoms (*choti elaichi*) | 3 tbsp / 12 gm | green coriander (*hara dhaniya*), chopped |
| Salt to taste | | | |
| ¼ tsp | saffron (*zafran*) | | |

## Method

1. Boil the water in a deep pan; add the meat and bring the water to the boil again. Blanch for 2-3 minutes and then drain the water. Cool the meat and wash under cold running water. Keep aside.
2. Put the blanched meat in a pan; add the pure ghee, onion purée, garlic, cloves, green cardamoms, salt, saffron, cooked yoghurt, turmeric and coriander powders. Mix well and cook until the ghee separates from the mixture.
3. Add just enough water so that when the meat is tender very little water remains. Sprinkle the black pepper powder and stir.
4. Serve hot, garnished with green coriander.

# Kishmish Korma

*Lamb cooked with plump raisins and saffron*

## Ingredients

| | | | |
|---|---|---|---|
| 600 gm | hind leg of lamb, cut into ½" x ½" x ½" cubes (the same size as the raisins) | Salt to taste | |
| | | 3 tbsp / 45 ml | garlic (*lasan*) water (see p. 17) |
| | | 1 tbsp / 20 gm | sugar |
| 10 | green cardamoms (*choti elaichi*) | 2 tbsp / 12 gm | tamarind (*imli*), boiled in 4 tbsp water, extract |
| 6 | cinnamon (*dalchini*) sticks, 1" each | ¼ tsp | saffron (*zafran*), ground and added to 1 tbsp warm water |
| ¾ cup / 145 gm | pure (*desi*) ghee | | |
| 3 | cloves (*laung*) | 1 cup / 100 gm | raisins (*kishmish*), fried until plump |
| 4 cups / 800 ml | water | | |

## Method

1. Add the meat to the boiling water and boil for 1 minute. Drain the water and keep aside.
2. In a shallow pan, add the blanched meat, green cardamoms, cinnamon sticks, pure ghee and cloves. Stir-fry for 2-3 minutes. Pour in the water and salt. Bring the mixture to the boil and add the garlic water, sugar and tamarind extract. Cook until the meat is tender and no water remains.
3. Add the saffron and raisins. Mix well and heat through.

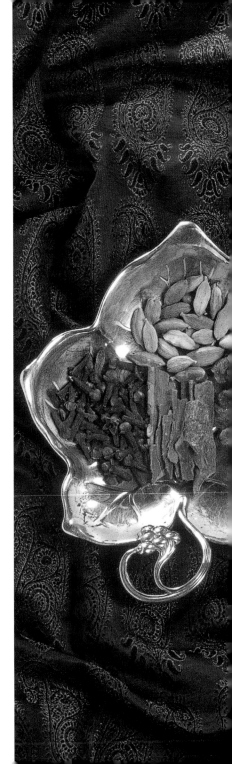

# Rogan Josh

*The original recipe from the valley*

## Ingredients

| | | | | |
|---|---|---|---|---|
| 1 kg | meat, cut into pieces | 4 tsp / 8 gm | Kashmiri red chilli |
| 15 cups / 3 lt | water | | powder, dissolved in |
| 2¼ tsp / 9 gm | salt | | 1 cup water |
| 1 tbsp / 18 gm | garlic (*lasan*), | ½ tsp / ½ gm | saffron (*zafran*), |
| | ground | | ground and added to |
| 1 cup / 190 gm | pure (*desi*) ghee | | 2 tbsp warm water |
| 4 | cloves (*laung*) | 1 cup / 200 ml | dry cockscomb |
| 8 | green cardamoms | | (*mawal*) flowers, |
| | (*choti elaichi*) | | heated with 1 cup |
| 5 tsp / 10 gm | turmeric (*haldi*) | | water (see p.17) |
| | powder | ¼ tsp | black pepper (*kali* |
| 2 tbsp / 50 gm | onion paste, fried | | *mirch*) powder |

## Method

1. Boil the meat in the water; remove the scum with a ladle until the water is clear. Add the salt and garlic. Boil until the meat is half done. Remove from heat and take out the pieces of meat. Wash them in a pan of cold water. Keep the meat aside. Then strain the water through a fine sieve and collect it in another pan. Return this pan to the heat and bring the water to the boil. Add the meat.

2. Meanwhile, heat the ghee in a pan; add the cloves, and sauté until they crackle. Remove from heat, sprinkle 1 tbsp water (carefully) and cover.

3. To the boiling water, add the green cardamoms, turmeric powder, clove-flavoured ghee and onion paste. Boil for another 10 minutes. Stir in the red chilli water. Reduce heat and cook covered until the meat is tender.

4. Add the cockscomb flower extract, saffron water and black pepper powder. Mix well and bring rapidly to the boil.

# Hindi Rogan Josh

*A variation of the original recipe*

## Ingredients

| | | | |
|---|---|---|---|
| 1 kg | neck of lamb, cut into pieces | Salt to taste | |
| 5 cups / 1 lt | water | 5 | bay leaves (*tej patta*) |
| 1½ tbsp / 36 gm | ginger (*adrak*), julienned | 2 tbsp / 24 gm | onion, grated |
| 6 | green cardamoms (*choti elaichi*) | 2 cups / 400 ml | cooked yoghurt (see p. 17) |
| | | 1 cup / 190 gm | pure (*desi*) ghee |
| 6 | cinnamon (*dalchini*) sticks, 1" each | ½ cup | Kashmiri red chilli powder, dissolved in 5 cups water |
| 6 | cloves (*laung*) | 2 tsp / 4 gm | turmeric (*haldi*) powder |
| 6 | black cardamoms (*bari elaichi*) | 2 tsp / 6 gm | tamarind (*imli*), boiled in 3 tbsp water, strained, extract |

## Method

1. Blanch the meat in boiling water for 1 minute. Drain the water and wash the meat in cold water.
2. Mix the blanched meat with ginger, green cardamoms, cinnamon sticks, cloves, black cardamoms, salt, bay leaves, onions, cooked yoghurt and ghee in a pan. Fry the meat until the water has dried up.
3. Add 1 cup red chilli water, stir until it is completely absorbed and the ghee rises to the surface. Repeat this process adding a cup at a time, till all the red chilli water is used up.
4. In another pan, add 6 cups water, turmeric powder, tamarind extract and the meat mixture. Reduce the heat to low, cover and simmer until the meat is tender, and very little water remains.

# Ghushtaba

*Pounded mutton balls in a delicious yoghurt-based gravy*

## Ingredients

| | | | |
|---|---|---|---|
| 10 | *ghushtaba* (see p.17) | 6 | black cardamoms (*bari elaichi*) |
| 5 cups / 1 lt | cooked yoghurt (see p. 17) | | |
| ⅓ cup / 65 gm | pure (*desi*) ghee | 6 | cloves (*laung*) |
| 4 cups / 800 ml | stock, made with 4-5 bones boiled in 6 cups water, covered, for 45 minutes, strained. | 3 tsp / 6 gm | fennel (*saunf*) powder |
| | | 3 tsp / 6 gm | dry ginger powder (*sonth*) |
| | | ¼ cup / 50 ml | garlic (*lasan*) water, (see p. 17) |
| | | 1 tbsp / 25 gm | onion paste, fried |
| 8 | green cardamoms (*choti elaichi*) | Salt to taste | |
| | | ¼ tsp | dry mint (*pudina*) leaves |

## Method

1. In a pan, add the *ghushtaba*, cooked yoghurt, pure ghee, and stock; bring to a rapid boil. Add the green and black cardamoms, cloves, fennel powder and dry ginger powders. Cover the pan and continue to boil for 10-12 minutes.

2. Add the garlic water and salt; boil for a further 10-12 minutes. Pour in more water, if required, to maintain a soup-like consistency. Add the onion paste and salt. Cook until the *ghushtaba* is tender to the touch and the gravy has thickened.

3. Sprinkle the dry mint leaves and heat through.

*(See picture on page 6)*

# Rista

*Pounded mutton balls flavoured in a saffron-flavoured gravy*

## Ingredients

| | | | |
|---|---|---|---|
| 10 | *rista* (see p. 17) | 1½ tbsp / 37 gm | onion paste, fried |
| 12 cups / 2400 ml | stock, made with 8 bones boiled in 15 cups water, covered, for 45 minutes, strained | 2 tsp / 4 gm | Kashmiri red chilli powder, dissolved in 1 cup water |
| 12 | green cardamoms (*choti elaichi*) | ¼ tsp | saffron (*zafran*) |
| | | ½ cup / 100 ml | dry cockscomb (*maval*) flowers, heated with ½ cup water, extract (see p. 17) |
| 6 | cloves (*laung*) | | |
| 3½ tsp / 7 gm | turmeric (*haldi*) powder | ¼ tsp | black pepper (*kali mirch*) powder |
| ½ cup / 95 gm | pure (*desi*) ghee | | |
| ¼ cup / 50 ml | garlic (*lasan*) water, (see p. 17) | Salt to taste | |

## Method

1. In a pan, add the *rista*, stock, green cardamoms, cloves, turmeric powder, ghee, garlic water, onion paste, red chilli water and salt. Bring the mixture to the boil. Mix well and cook covered until the *rista* is tender and the gravy is of a soup-like consistency.
2. Add the saffron, cockscomb flower extract, black pepper powder and salt. Mix well.

# Palak Rista

*Meat balls cooked with spinach*

## Ingredients

| | | | |
|---|---|---|---|
| 500 gm | spinach (*palak*) washed, boiled | Salt to taste | |
| 15 | *rista* (see p. 17) | 3 tsp / 6 gm | Kashmiri red chilli powder, dissolved in 1 cup water |
| 1 tbsp / 18 gm | garlic (*lasan*), ground | ¼ cup / 50 ml | dry cockscomb (*mawal*) flowers, heated with 1 cup water, extract (see p. 17) |
| 17 cups / 3400 ml | stock (see p. 38) | | |
| 4 tsp / 8 gm | turmeric (*haldi*) powder | | |
| 6 | green cardamoms (*choti elaichi*) | 1 tsp / 2 gm | black cardamom (*bari elaichi*) powder |
| 4 | cinnamon (*dalchini*) sticks, 2" each | ¼ tsp | black pepper (*kali mirch*) powder |
| 2 tsp / 4 gm | dry ginger powder (*sonth*) | ½ tsp / 1 gm | black cumin seeds (*shah jeera*) |

## Method

1. Squeeze and drain out the water from the boiled spinach. Then chop them coarsely. Fry them in refined oil with the garlic until the spinach is crisp. Keep aside.

2. Heat the *rista* with the stock, turmeric powder, green cardamoms, cinnamon sticks, dry ginger powder and salt in a pan, and mix well. Bring the mixture to a rapid boil and cook for 20-24 minutes.

3. Add the red chilli water and cook for another 20 minutes. Add the cockscomb flower extract, spinach, and 2 cups water. Mix well. Bring the mixture to the boil. Reduce heat and cook till very little gravy remains and the ghee separates from the mixture. Add the black cardamom powder, pepper powder, cumin seeds and salt. Mix well.

# Naat Yakkhn

*Lamb cooked in yoghurt*

## Ingredients

| | | | | |
|---|---|---|---|---|
| 700 gm | assorted lamb, cut into large pieces | 1 cup / 200 ml | cooked yoghurt (see p. 17) |
| 12½ cups / 2½ lt | water | 2 tsp / 4 gm | Kashmiri red chilli powder, dissolved in ½ cup water |
| 1¼ tsp / 7½ gm | garlic (*lasan*), ground | | |
| Salt to taste | | ⅓ cup / 65 gm | pure (*desi*) ghee |
| 8 | green cardamoms (*choti elaichi*) | ½ cup / 100 ml | dry cockscomb (*mawal*) flowers, heated with ½ cup water, extract (see p. 17) |
| 4 | black cardamoms (*bari elaichi*) | | |
| 6 | cloves (*laung*) | | |
| 2 tsp / 4 gm | turmeric (*haldi*) powder | ½ tsp / 1 gm | black cumin seeds (*shah jeera*) |
| ½ tsp / 1 gm | dry ginger powder (*sonth*) | ½ tsp / 1 gm | dry mint (*pudina*) leaves |
| 1½ tbsp / 37 gm | onion paste, fried | | |

## Method

1. Bring the water to the boil in a deep pan. Add the lamb and remove the scum that rises to the surface. When the water is clear, add the garlic and continue to boil for 4-5 minutes. Add the salt and cook until the lamb is half done.
2. Add the green and black cardamoms, cloves, turmeric powder, dry ginger powder, onion paste, cooked yoghurt, red chilli water and ghee. Mix well, reduce heat and cook covered until the lamb is tender.
3. Add the cockscomb flower extract and black cumin seeds. Mix well. Sprinkle dry mint leaves.

# Maaz Yakkhn

*Meat flavoured with aniseed and dry ginger powder*

## Ingredients

| | | | | |
|---|---|---|---|---|
| 1 kg | assorted meat pieces | 2½ tsp / 5 gm | aniseed (*moti saunf*) powder |
| 25 cups / 5 lt | water | 2½ tsp / 5 gm | dry ginger powder (*sonth*) |
| 1½ tbsp / 27 gm | garlic (*lasan*), ground | ½ cup / 95 gm | pure (*desi*) ghee |
| Salt to taste | | 4 cups / 800 ml | cooked yoghurt (see p. 17) |
| 10 | green cardamoms (*choti elaichi*) | 1½ tbsp / 37 gm | onion paste, fried |
| 4 | black cardamoms (*bari elaichi*) | 1 tsp / 2 gm | black cumin seeds (*shah jeera*) |
| 5 | cloves (*laung*) | 1½ tsp / 3 gm | dry mint (*pudina*) leaves |

## Method

1. In a deep pan, boil the water with meat. Remove the scum that rises from time to time. When the water is clean, add the garlic and salt and cook until the meat is half done.
2. Remove the pan from the heat, take out the meat pieces and wash them in cold water. Keep aside. Strain the stock and collect it in a deep pan. Add the meat and bring the mixture to the boil.
3. Add the green and black cardamoms, cloves, aniseed powder, dry ginger powder, ghee, cooked yoghurt and onion paste. Mix well. Cover with a lid and continue to cook until the meat is tender and the gravy is of a sauce-like consistency.
4. Sprinkle the black cumin seeds and dry mint leaves. Mix well.

# Aab Gosh

*Meat in a thick milk gravy*

## Ingredients

| | | | |
|---|---|---|---|
| 1 kg | meat, cut into pieces from the shoulder and putt | 6 | cloves (*laung*) |
| 18 cups / 3600 ml water | | 8 | green cardamoms (*choti elaichi*) |
| 2 tsp / 12 gm | garlic (*lasan*), ground | 1 tsp / 6 gm | onion paste, fried |
| 2 tbsp / 8 gm | aniseed (*moti saunf*) powder | 10 cups / 2 lt | milk, boiled until it is reduced to 500 ml or 2 cups |
| Salt to taste | | | |
| ½ cup / 95 gm | pure (*desi*) ghee | | |

## Method

1. Boil the meat in the water. Remove the scum with a ladle until the water is clear. Add the garlic, fennel powder and salt. Cook until the meat is half done.
2. Remove the pan from the heat and keep aside to cool. Strain the stock and collect it in another pan. Wash the meat in cold water and keep aside.
3. Heat the ghee in a small pan; add the cloves. Sauté them until they crackle. Sprinkle 1 tbsp water carefully, and cover the pan with a lid.
4. Add the meat to the strained stock with the green cardamoms, clove-flavoured ghee and onion paste. Bring the mixture to the boil. Reduce heat and cook covered till the meat is tender and very little water remains.
5. Add the reduced milk and mix well. Heat through.

*(See picture on page 2)*

# Methi Maaz

*A Kashmiri delicacy*

## Ingredients

| | | | |
|---|---|---|---|
| 2 | stomachs | 1 tsp / 2 gm | Kashmiri red chilli powder, dissolved in ½ cup water |
| 2 | intestines of a goat | | |
| ½ cup / 100 ml | garlic (*lasan*), ground | ½ cup / 100 ml | dry cockscomb (*mawal*) flowers, heated with 1 cup water, extract (see p.17) |
| Salt to taste | | | |
| 8 | green cardamoms (*choti elaichi*) | 20 tsp / 10 gm | dry fenugreek leaves (*kasoori methi*) |
| 6 | black cardamoms (*bari elaichi*) | | |
| 4 tsp / 8 gm | turmeric (*haldi*) powder | 1 cup / 190 gm | pure (*desi*) ghee |
| 2 tsp / 4 gm | dry ginger powder (*sonth*) | 1 tsp / 2 gm | black cardamom (*bari elaichi*) powder |
| 4 | cinnamon (*dalchini*) sticks, 1" each | ¼ tsp | black pepper (*kali mirch*) powder |
| 1 tbsp / 18 gm | garlic (*lasan*) paste | | |

## Method

1. Cut open the stomachs and intestines and wash under running water at least 5-6 times.
2. Boil the stomachs for 2-3 minutes and then drain the water. Remove the outer rough membrane with your hands until the surface is smooth.
3. Boil 20 cups water in a deep pan; add the stomachs and intestines. Remove the scum that rises. When the water is clear, add the garlic and salt. Boil until half done. Remove from heat and keep aside to cool. Reserve the stock. When cool, chop the stomachs and intestines coarsely into small rectangular pieces and strips.
4. In a deep pan, heat 15 cups of the reserved stock. Add the chopped meat, cardamoms, turmeric and dry ginger powders, cinnamon sticks and garlic paste. Boil for 25 minutes.
5. Mix in the red chilli water and boil for 20 minutes more. Reduce heat to low and simmer for 25 minutes or till the meat is tender. Add a little water, if required.
6. Meanwhile, boil the dry fenugreek leaves in 1 cup water and drain. Heat the pure ghee; fry the drained fenugreek leaves. To the meat mixture, add the cockscomb flower extract, fried fenugreek leaves, black cardamom and pepper powders. Mix well.

# Nadir Gadh

*Fish fillets cooked with lotus stems*

## Ingredients

| | | | |
|---|---|---|---|
| ½ kg | firm, white river fish fillets | 6 | green cardamoms (*choti* |
| ½ kg | lotus stems (*kamal kakri*), | | *elaichi*) |
| | cut diagonally ½" apart, | 2 tsp / 4 gm | dry ginger powder (*sonth*) |
| | thoroughly washed | 2 tsp / 4 gm | turmeric (*haldi*) powder |
| 1 cup / 170 ml | refined oil | 4 | cinnamon (*dalchini*) sticks, |
| 1 tbsp / 18 gm | garlic (*lasan*), ground | | 1" each |
| 1 tbsp / 15 gm | ver paste (see p. 17) | Salt to taste | |
| 2 tsp / 4 gm | Kashmiri red chilli powder, | 1½ tbsp / 37 gm | onion paste, fried |
| | dissolved in 1 cup water | ¼ cup / 50 ml | dry cockscomb (*mawal*) |
| 8 cups / 1600 ml | water | | flowers, heated with 1 cup |
| 5 | cloves (*laung*) | | water, extract (see p.17) |
| 5 | black cardamoms (*bari* | ½ tsp / 1 gm | black cumin seeds (*shah* |
| | *elaichi*) | | *jeera*) |

## Method

1. Fry the fish in refined oil until reddish brown. Remove with a slotted spoon and drain the excess oil on absorbent kitchen towels.

2. Heat the refined oil in a deep pan; add the lotus stems and the garlic. Fry until brown specks appear on the stems.

3. Add the ver paste and red chilli water. Keep stirring until all the water has dried up and the oil rises to the surface. Reduce the heat and carefully add the water, cloves, black and green cardamoms, dry ginger powder, turmeric powder, cinnamon sticks, salt and onion paste. Bring the mixture to the boil. Then lower the heat and simmer for 10-12 minutes or until the stems are tender.

4. Add the fried fish and the cockscomb flower extract. Bring the mixture to the boil again, stirring slowly and making sure that the fish does not break. Sprinkle the black cumin seeds and cook till it is of a soup like-consistency.

# Mugh Gadh

*Fish cooked with radish*

## Ingredients

| | | | |
|---|---|---|---|
| 1 kg | firm, white river fish, boneless, cut into 1½" x 2" x 1½" cubes with skin, washed | 8 | green cardamoms (*choti elaichi*) |
| | | 4 | black cardamoms (*bari elaichi*) |
| 750 gm | radish (*mooli*), sliced into round discs and then halved | 5 | cloves (*laung*) |
| | | 2 tsp / 4 gm | dry ginger powder (*sonth*) |
| 1 cup / 170 ml | refined oil | 3 tsp / 6 gm | turmeric (*haldi*) powder |
| 1 tbsp / 18 gm | garlic (*lasan*), ground | Salt to taste | |
| 2 tsp / 4 gm | Kashmiri red chilli powder, dissolved in 1 cup water | 1½ tbsp / 37 gm onion paste, fried | |
| | | ½ tsp / 1 gm | black cumin seeds (*shah jeera*) |
| 1 tsp / 5 gm | ver paste (see p.17) | ½ tsp / 1 gm | black pepper powder (*kali mirch*) |
| 6 cups / 1200 ml | water | | |
| 4 | cinnamon (*dalchini*) sticks, 1" each | 1 tsp / 2 gm | black cardamom seeds (*bari elaichi*), powdered |

## Method

1. Fry the fish in refined oil until reddish brown. Remove with a slotted spoon and drain the excess oil on absorbent kitchen towels. Keep aside.
2. Sprinkle salt on the radish and keep aside for half an hour. Then wash and keep aside.
3. Heat the refined oil in a wok; add the garlic and the radish. Fry until the radish turn reddish brown on the edges.
4. Mix in the red chilli water and ver paste. Pour in the water and bring the mixture to the boil. Add the cinnamon sticks, green and black cardamoms, cloves, dry ginger powder, turmeric powder, salt and onion paste. Mix well and cook for 10-12 minutes.
5. Add the fried fish and boil rapidly for 2 minutes. Make sure that the fish pieces do not break. Add black cumin seeds, black pepper powder and black cardamom seed powder. Mix well.

# Ruwagan Gadh

*Fish cooked delicately in a tomato gravy*

## Ingredients

| | | | |
|---|---|---|---|
| ½ kg | firm, white river fish, cut into cubes | 2 tsp / 4 gm | turmeric (*haldi*) powder |
| 1 cup / 170 ml | refined oil | 4 | cinnamon (*dalchini*) sticks, 1" each |
| 2 cups / 400 ml | tomato purée | Salt to taste | |
| 1 tbsp / 15 gm | ver paste (see p. 17) | 1½ tbsp / 37 gm | onion paste, fried |
| 1 tbsp / 18 gm | garlic (*lasan*), ground | 2 tsp / 4 gm | Kashmiri red chilli powder, dissolved in 1 cup water |
| 5 cups / 1 lt | water | | |
| 1 tsp / 2 gm | dry ginger powder (*sonth*) | 1 tsp / 2 gm | black pepper (*kali mirch*) powder |
| 8 | cloves (*laung*) | | |
| 5 | green cardamoms (*choti elaichi*) | 1 tsp / 2 gm | black cardamom (*bari elaichi*) seeds, powdered |
| 6 | black cardamoms (*bari elaichi*) | ½ tsp / 1 gm | black cumin seeds (*shah jeera*) |

## Method

1. Fry the fish in refined oil until reddish brown. Remove with a slotted spoon and drain the excess oil on absorbent kitchen towels. Keep aside.

2. Heat the refined oil in a pan; add the tomato purée, ver paste and garlic; fry for 2-3 minutes. Add the water, dry ginger powder, cloves, green and black cardamoms, turmeric powder, cinnamon sticks, salt, onion paste and the red chilli water. Mix well and bring the mixture to the boil. Continue to boil on high heat for 5 minutes.

3. Add the fried fish, reduce heat to low and bring the mixture to the boil. Add the black pepper powder, black cardamom powder and black cumin seeds. Mix well and let the mixture simmer until the oil rises to the surface.

# Haakh Gadh

*Fish cooked with distinct Kashmiri spinach*

## Ingredients

| | | | |
|---|---|---|---|
| ½ kg | firm, white river fish, cut into cubes | 2 tsp / 4 gm | Kashmiri red chilli powder, dissolved in 1 cup water |
| ½ kg | Kashmiri spinach (*haakh*), washed well | Salt to taste | |
| 15 cups / 3 lt | water | 1 cup / 190 gm | pure (*desi*) ghee |
| 1 tbsp / 18 gm | garlic (*lasan*), ground | ½ cup / 120 gm | onions, sliced |
| 2 tbsp / 4 gm | turmeric (*haldi*) powder | 1 tsp / 2 gm | Kashmiri red chilli powder |
| 5 | green cardamoms (*choti elaichi*) | 1 tsp / 5 gm | ver paste (see p.17) |
| | | ½ tsp / 1 gm | black cumin seeds (*shah jeera*) |

## Method

1. Fry the fish in refined oil until reddish brown. Remove with a slotted spoon and drain the excess oil on absorbent kitchen towels. Keep aside.

2. Bring the water to the boil in a deep pan with garlic, turmeric powder, green cardamoms, red chilli water and salt. Now add the Kashmiri spinach and boil it again. Reduce the heat, and cook until the leaves are tender and very little water remains.

3. In another pan, heat the pure ghee and fry the onions. Mix in the red chillies, ver paste and the fried fish. Add the Kashmiri spinach mixture. Sprinkle black cumin seeds and mix well.

# Kukkur Lahabdar Kabab Ruwagan

*Chicken kebabs in a rich tomato gravy*

## Ingredients

| | | | |
|---|---|---|---|
| 1 kg | thighs and drumsticks of chicken, boneless | 4 | cinnamon (*dalchini*) sticks, 1" each |
| 3 tsp / 6 gm | Kashmiri red chilli powder | 6 | black cardamoms (*bari elaichi*) |
| 3 tsp / 12 gm | salt | 3 tsp / 6 gm | turmeric (*haldi*) powder |

**For the paste:**

| | | | |
|---|---|---|---|
| ½ tsp / 1 gm | black cardamom (*bari elaichi*) powder | 2 tbsp / 50 gm | onion paste, fried |
| 1½ tsp / 3 gm | green coriander (*hara dhaniya*), chopped | 5 tsp / 10 gm | Kashmiri red chilli powder, dissolved in 1 cup water |
| 1 tsp / 2 gm | black cumin seeds (*shah jeera*) | 1 cup / 200 ml | dry cockscomb (*mawal*) flowers, heated in 1½ cups water (see p. 17) |
| 2 tsp / 4 gm | turmeric (*haldi*) powder | | |
| 1 tsp / 2 gm | dry ginger powder (*sonth*) | ¾ tsp | saffron (*zafran*), ground and then added to 2 tbsp warm water |
| 1 tsp / 2 gm | dry mint (*pudina*) leaves | | |
| 2 | eggs, lightly beaten | ½ cup / 100 ml | garlic (*lasan*) water (see p. 17) |

**For the gravy:**

| | | | |
|---|---|---|---|
| 1 cup / 190 gm | pure (*desi*) ghee | 1½ tsp / 3 gm | dry mint (*pudina*) leaves |
| 3 cups / 600 ml | tomato purée, diluted with 3 cups water, 2 tsp salt and 1 tbsp garlic water | 1 tsp / 2 gm | black cumin seeds (*shah jeera*) |
| 10 | green cardamoms (*choti elaichi*) | | |

**For the garnish:**

| | | |
|---|---|---|
| ¼ cup / 60 gm | cashew nuts (*kaju*), halved |
| 3 tsp / 6 gm | dry ginger powder (*sonth*) | 1 tbsp / 4 gm | green coriander (*hara dhaniya*), finely chopped |

# *Method*

1. Coarsely chop the chicken with the red chillies. Add the salt and mix well. Keep in the freezer for 1 hour.
2. Remove the chicken from the freezer and pass it through a mincing machine twice.
3. **For the paste**, mix all the ingredients together and grind them to a smooth paste. Mix this paste with the chicken. Divide the mixture into 8 equal-sized portions and keep aside on a greased tray.
4. Moisten hands in ice-cold water and roll each portion to form smooth balls. Then moisten hands again and slowly flatten the balls to make a kebab in the shape of a flat boat. Repeat this process till all the kebabs have been shaped. Keep aside.
5. **For the gravy,** heat the ghee in a heavy-bottomed pan; add the tomato purée, green cardamoms, dry ginger powder, cinnamon sticks, black cardamoms and turmeric powder. Bring the mixture to the boil and then add the onion paste. Mix well and lower the kebabs, making sure that they do not break. Cook on medium heat for 45 minutes or until the kebabs are tender, stirring occasionally.
6. Add the red chilli water, cockscomb flower extract, saffron water, garlic water, dry mint leaves and black cumin seeds. Mix well and cook for a further 5-7 minutes.
7. Serve hot, garnished with cashew nuts and green coriander.

# Kukkur Rogan Josh

*Saffron-flavoured chicken*

## Ingredients

| | | | |
|---|---|---|---|
| 1 | chicken, cut into 8 pieces | 2 tbsp / 50 gm | onion paste, fried |
| Refined oil for frying | | 4 tsp / 8 gm | Kashmiri red chilli powder, |
| 1 cup / 190 gm | pure (*desi*) ghee | | dissolved in 1 cup water |
| 4 | cloves (*laung*) | ½ tsp / ½ gm | saffron (*zafran*), ground and |
| 15 cups / 3 lt | water | | added to 2 tbsp warm water |
| 2¼ tsp / 9 gm | salt | 1 cup / 200 ml | dry cockscomb (*mawal*) |
| ½ cup / 100 ml | garlic (*lasan*) water (see p. 17) | | flowers, heated with 1 cup |
| 8 | green cardamoms (*choti* | | water, extract (see p. 17) |
| | *elaichi*) | ¼ tsp | black pepper (*kali mirch*) |
| 5 tsp / 10 gm | turmeric (*haldi*) powder | | powder |

## Method

1. Heat the refined oil in a wok (*kadhai*); fry the chicken until light brown in colour. Remove and drain the excess oil on absorbent kitchen towels. Keep aside.

2. Meanwhile, heat the pure ghee in a pan; add the cloves and sauté them till they crackle. Remove the pan from the heat; very carefully sprinkle 1 tbsp water, and then cover the pan with a lid.

3. Mix the fried chicken with the water, salt, garlic water, green cardamoms, turmeric powder, clove-flavoured ghee and onion paste. Bring the mixture to the boil.

4. Add the red chilli water and mix well. On a medium heat, with the pan covered, cook the chicken until it is tender. Stir in the cockscomb flower extract, saffron water and black pepper powder. Bring it to a rapid boil. Serve hot.

(See picture on page 8)

# Dum Olav

*Potatoes in a spicy red gravy*

### Ingredients

| | | | |
|---|---|---|---|
| 750 gm | potatoes, unpeeled, 1" x 1½" pieces | ½ cup / 100 ml | cooked yoghurt (see p. 17) |
| 1 cup / 170 ml | refined oil | 3 tsp / 6 gm | Kashmiri red chilli powder, dissolved in 1 cup water |
| 8 | black cardamoms (*bari elaichi*) | | |
| 8 | green cardamoms (*choti elaichi*) | 1 tbsp / 25 gm | onion paste, fried |
| | | Salt to taste | |
| 5 | cloves (*laung*) | 1½ tsp / 3 gm | turmeric (*haldi*) powder |
| 5 | cinnamon (*dalchini*) sticks, 2" each | ¼ cup / 50 ml | dry cockscomb (*mawal*) flowers, heated with ½ cup water, extract (see p. 17) |
| 3 tbsp / 12 gm | dry ginger powder (*sonth*) | | |
| 3 tbsp / 12 gm | aniseed (*moti saunf*) powder | | |
| 5 | bay leaves (*tej patta*) | ¼ tsp | black cumin seeds (*shah jeera*) |
| 1½ tsp / 9 gm | garlic (*lasan*), ground | | |

### Method

1. Boil the potatoes until tender. Keep aside to cool. Peel and pierce through them with a toothpick. Heat 1 cup refined oil and fry the potatoes on very low heat until they are reddish brown. Stir occasionally while frying. Remove and drain on kitchen towels.

2. In a pan, add the cardamoms, cloves, cinnamon sticks, dry ginger powder, aniseed powder, bay leaves, garlic, cooked yoghurt, red chilli water, onion paste and salt. Stir to make a homogenous paste.

3. Pour in 3 cups water, bring the mixture to the boil and cook for 3-4 minutes. Add the potatoes and turmeric powder. Reduce heat to low and cook covered for 5 minutes more. Add the cockscomb flower extract and cook until the oil separates. Mix in the black cumin seeds.

# Haakh

*Distinct Kashmiri spinach*

## Ingredients

| | | | |
|---|---|---|---|
| 500 gm | Kashmiri spinach (*haakh*), leaves without stems, washed under cold running water | | powder, dissolved in 1 cup water |

**For the tempering:**

| | | | |
|---|---|---|---|
| 15 cups / 3 lt | water | ½ cup / 85 ml | refined oil |
| 8 tsp / 16 gm | turmeric (*haldi*) powder | ¼ cup / 60 gm | onions, chopped |
| | | 5 tsp / 10 gm | Kashmiri red chilli powder |
| 2 tsp / 12 gm | garlic (*lasan*), ground | 1 tsp / 2 gm | black cumin seeds (*shah jeera*) |
| Salt to taste | | ¼ tsp | dry ginger powder (*sonth*) |
| 2 tsp / 4 gm | Kashmiri red chilli | | |

## Method

1. Boil the water in a deep pan; add the Kashmiri spinach, turmeric powder, garlic, salt and red chilli water. Mix well. Bring the mixture back to the boil again, cover the pan with a lid and continue to boil until the spinach is tender and very little water remains.
2. **For the tempering**, heat the refined oil in a pan; add the onions and sauté till golden brown. Remove the pan from the heat and add the red chilli powder. Stir and add this tempering to the cooked spinach mixture. Mix in the black cumin seeds and dry ginger powder.

# Palak Chhaman

*Spinach with cottage cheese*

## Ingredients

| | | | |
|---|---|---|---|
| 1 kg | spinach (*palak*), leaves only, washed, boiled, drained | 6 | cinnamon (*dalchini*) sticks, 2" each |
| 500 gm | cottage cheese (*paneer*), cut into 1½" x 1½" x 1½" cubes | 1 tsp / 2 gm | dry ginger powder (*sonth*) |
| 1 cup / 170 ml | refined oil | 2 tsp / 4 gm | Kashmiri red chilli powder, dissolved in 1 cup water |
| 1 tbsp / 18 gm | garlic (*lasan*), ground | Salt to taste | |
| 7 cups / 1400 ml | water | ½ tsp / 1 gm | green cardamom (*choti elaichi*) seed, powdered |
| 8 | green cardamoms (*choti elaichi*) | ¼ tsp | black pepper (*kali mirch*) powder |
| 6 | black cardamoms (*bari elaichi*) | ½ tsp / 1 gm | black cumin seeds (*shah jeera*) |
| 3 tsp / 6 gm | turmeric (*haldi*) powder | | |

## Method

1. Squeeze out as much water as possible from the spinach leaves with your hands. Chop the leaves coarsely.

2. Fry the cottage cheese in refined oil until light brown. Remove with a slotted spoon and immerse them in water. Keep aside.

3. Heat the refined oil in a deep pan; add the garlic and the boiled spinach. Mix well. Fry the spinach until the colour changes and all the water has evaporated.

4. Add the water, green and black cardamoms, turmeric powder, cinnamon sticks, dry ginger powder, red chilli water and salt. Bring the mixture to the boil and cook it until the water is reduced to half its original quantity. Add the drained, fried cottage cheese. Cook till all the water has been absorbed.

5. Add the green cardamom powder, black pepper powder and cumin seeds. Mix well.

# Manje Haakh

*Knol-khol greens*

### Ingredients

| | | | |
|---|---|---|---|
| 500 gm | knol-khol (*karam*), peeled, diced | 6 cups / 1200 ml | warm water |
| 500 gm | knol-khol (*karam*) leaves only | 2 tsp / 4 gm | turmeric (*haldi*) powder |
| 10 cups / 2 lt | water | 1 tsp / 4 gm | salt |
| 1 cup / 190 gm | pure (*desi*) ghee | 1¼ tsp / 7½ gm | garlic (*lasan*), ground |
| 2 tsp / 4 gm | Kashmiri red chilli powder, dissolved in 1 cup water | 1 tsp / 2 gm | black cumin seeds (*shah jeera*) |

### Method

1. Sprinkle some salt on the knol-khol and keep aside for 15 minutes. Then wash them well.
2. Wash and boil the knol-khol leaves for 2-3 minutes. Drain, and when cool, chop them coarsely.
3. Heat the pure ghee in a pan; fry the diced knol-khol until it changes colour. Add the knol-khol leaves and fry for another 3-5 minutes. Add the red chilli water and the warm water. Bring the mixture to the boil and then reduce the heat.
4. Add the turmeric powder, salt and garlic. Cover the pan and simmer the knol-khol mixture until it is tender and very little water remains.
5. Sprinkle black cumin seeds and mix well.

# Ruwagan Chhaman

*Cottage cheese in a flavourful tomato gravy*

### Ingredients

| | | | |
|---|---|---|---|
| 1 kg | fried cottage cheese (*paneer*), cut into 2"x1½"x1" cubes | 4 | black cardamoms (*bari elaichi*) |
| 3 cups / 600 ml | tomato purée, diluted with 3 cups water, 2 tsp salt and 1 tbsp garlic water | 1 cup / 190 gm | pure (*desi*) ghee |
| | | 2 tsp / 4 gm | Kashmiri red chilli powder, dissolved in ¾ cup water |
| 8 | green cardamoms (*choti elaichi*) | ¾ cup / 150 ml | dry cockscomb flowers (*mawal*), heated with 1 cup water, extract (see p. 17) |
| 4 | cinnamon (*dalchini*) sticks, 1" each | | |
| 2 tsp / 4 gm | turmeric (*haldi*) powder | 2 tsp / 4 gm | dry mint (*pudina*) leaves |
| 2 tsp / 4 gm | dry ginger powder (*sonth*) | 1 tsp / 2 gm | black cumin seeds (*shah jeera*) |
| 1½ tsp / 9 gm | onion paste, fried | | Salt to taste |

### Method

1. In a pan, add the tomato purée mixture, green cardamoms, cinnamon sticks, turmeric powder, dry ginger powder, onion paste, black cardamoms, pure ghee, red chilli water and 5 cups water. Cook the mixture until it is of a sauce-like consistency.
2. Add the cockscomb flower extract and bring the mixture back to the boil. Add the fried cottage cheese after first immersing it in cold water. Cook until it is well blended with the sauce.
3. Add the dry mint leaves and black cumin seeds, and cook for another 5 minutes.

# Manje Kael

*Knol-khol prepared in onion gravy*

## Ingredients

| | | | |
|---|---|---|---|
| 1 kg | knol-khol (*karam*), diced | | powder, dissolved in ½ cup water |
| 2 tsp / 8 gm | salt | 2 tsp / 4 gm | turmeric (*haldi*) powder |
| ¾ cup / 180 gm | onions, sliced | | |
| 6 cups / 1200 ml | water | 1 tsp / 6 gm | garlic (*lasan*), ground |
| 10 | green cardamoms (*choti elaichi*) | 1 cup / 200 ml | cooked yoghurt (see p. 17) |
| 6 | black cardamoms (*bari elaichi*) | ½ cup / 100 ml | dry cockscomb (*mawal*) flowers, heated with ½ cup water, extract (see p. 17) |
| 1½ tsp / 3 gm | dry ginger powder (*sonth*) | | |
| 4 | cinnamon (*dalchini*) sticks, 1" each | 1 tsp / 2 gm | black cumin seeds (*shah jeera*) |
| 1½ tsp / 3 gm | Kashmiri red chilli | | |

## Method

1. Mix the salt with the knol-khol; keep aside for 5 minutes, wash and drain. Then fry the knol-khol in refined oil until light brown in colour. Remove with a slotted spoon and keep aside.
2. In the same oil, fry the onions until light brown. Drain and add to the fried knol-khol.
3. Heat the water in a deep pan and when hot, add the green and black cardamoms, dry ginger powder, cinnamon sticks, red chilli water, turmeric powder and garlic. Bring the mixture to the boil. Add the fried knol-khol mixture and cooked yoghurt.
4. Cook until all the water has evaporated. Add the cockscomb flower extract and stir well. Sprinkle black cumin seeds.

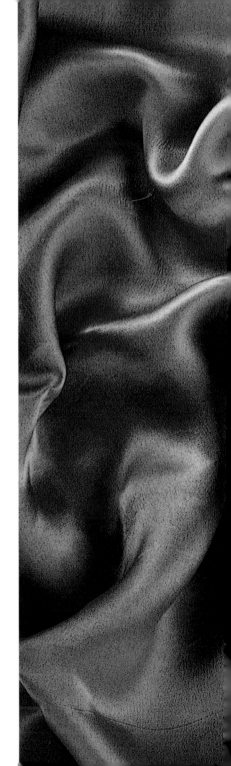

# Nadir Kabab

*Lotus stem patties*

## Ingredients

| | | | |
|---|---|---|---|
| 1 kg | lotus stems (*kamal kakri*), washed | 1 tsp / 2 gm | dry mint (*pudina*) powder |
| | | ¼ tsp | cinnamon (*dalchini*) powder |
| 1½ tbsp / 6 gm | green coriander (*hara dhaniya*), fresh, finely chopped | 1 tsp / 2 gm | Kashmiri red chilli powder |
| | | ¼ tsp | black pepper (*kali mirch*) powder |
| 1½ tbsp | green chillies, finely chopped | Salt to taste | |
| 2 tsp / 4 gm | black cumin seeds (*shah jeera*) | 6 tbsp / 90 gm | breadcrumbs |
| | | Refined oil for frying | |

## Method

1. Roast the lotus stems on a coal fire until large brown specks appear all over. Then peel the skin, chop the stems into thin slices and grind them to a coarse paste.
2. To this paste, add the green coriander, green chillies, black cumin seeds, dry mint powder, cinnamon powder, red chilli powder and black pepper powder. Mix well. Add the salt and breadcrumbs, and mix well again.
3. Divide the mixture into 25 balls, then flatten each ball and shape into a round patty.
4. Heat the refined oil in a pan; shallow fry the patties until light brown. Remove with a slotted spoon and drain the excess oil on absorbent kitchen towels.

*(See picture on page 5)*

# Haddar Yakkhn

*Mushrooms in a spicy gravy*

## Ingredients

| | | | |
|---|---|---|---|
| 1 kg | mushrooms, fresh, cut into 4 pieces each, washed well | Salt to taste | |
| ½ cup / 85 ml | refined oil | 1 tsp / 6 gm | garlic (*lasan*), ground |
| ¼ cup / 75 gm | onion paste | 1 cup / 200 ml | cooked yoghurt (see p. 17) |
| 10 | green cardamoms (*choti elaichi*) | 3 cups / 600 ml | water |
| | | 1½ tsp / 3 gm | dry ginger powder (*sonth*) |
| 4 | black cardamoms (*bari elaichi*) | 1½ tsp / 2 gm | coriander (*dhaniya*) powder |
| | | ¼ tsp | black cumin seeds (*shah jeera*) |
| 10 | cloves (*laung*) | ¼ tsp | black pepper (*kali mirch*) powder |
| 4 | cinnamon (*dalchini*) sticks, 1" each | ¼ tsp | dry mint (*pudina*) leaves |

## Method

1. Boil the mushrooms in water for 5-7 minutes. Drain and then wash in cold water.
2. In a pan, add the washed mushrooms, refined oil, onion paste, green and black cardamoms, cloves, cinnamon sticks, salt and garlic. Cook the mushrooms, stirring occasionally, until they are light brown in colour.
3. Add the cooked yoghurt and cook until the oil separates. Pour in the water, dry ginger and coriander powders. Mix well. Reduce the heat and simmer for 5-6 minutes to obtain a sauce-like consistency.
4. Add the black cumin seeds, black pepper powder and dry mint leaves, and mix well.

# Nadir Yakkhn

*Lotus stems cooked in a yoghurt gravy*

## Ingredients

| | | | |
|---|---|---|---|
| 1 kg | lotus stems (*kamal kakri*), cut diagonally into ¾" pieces, washed thoroughly | ⅓ cup / 64 gm | pure (*desi*) ghee |
| | | 2 tsp / 4 gm | aniseed (*moti saunf*) powder |
| | | 2 tsp / 4 gm | dry ginger powder (*sonth*) |
| 8 cups / 1600 ml | water | 2 cups / 400 ml | cooked yoghurt (see p. 17) |
| 4 | black cardamoms (*bari elaichi*) | ½ tbsp / 12 gm | onion paste, fried |
| 8 | green cardamoms (*choti elaichi*) | Salt to taste | |
| | | ¼ tsp | dry mint (*pudina*) leaves |
| 8 | cloves (*laung*) | | |
| 4 | cinnamon (*dalchini*) sticks, 1" each | ¼ tsp | black cumin seeds (*shah jeera*) |

## Method

1. Boil the water, add the lotus stems, and cook them until half done.
2. In another pan, add the black and green cardamoms, cloves, cinnamon sticks, ghee, aniseed powder, dry ginger powder, cooked yoghurt, onion paste and salt. Mix well and cook for 7-8 minutes.
3. Add the half-cooked lotus stems; reduce the heat and cook till tender.
4. Add the dry mint leaves and black cumin seeds. Mix well.

# Al Yakkhn

*Garlic-flavoured bottle gourd*

## *Ingredients*

| | | | |
|---|---|---|---|
| 1 kg | bottle gourd (*lauki*), peeled, cut into discs 1" apart, and then halved, with seeds removed | 4 | cinnamon (*dalchini*) sticks, 1" each |
| | | Salt to taste | |
| 10 cups / 2 lt | water | 1 tbsp / 15 ml | garlic (*lasan*) water (see p.17) |
| 2 tsp / 4 gm | dry ginger powder (*sonth*) | ½ tsp / 1 gm | turmeric (*haldi*) powder |
| 8 | green cardamoms (*choti elaichi*) | ⅓ cup / 65 gm | pure (*desi*) ghee |
| 3 | black cardamoms (*bari elaichi*) | 1 cup / 200 ml | cooked yoghurt (see p. 17) |
| 2 tsp / 3 gm | aniseed (*moti saunf*) | ¼ tsp | black cumin seeds (*shah jeera*) |

## *Method*

1. Add 1 tsp salt to the bottle gourd and mix well. Keep aside for 15 minutes.
2. Fry the bottle gourd in refined oil until reddish brown in colour. Remove with a slotted spoon and keep aside.
3. In a deep pan, boil the water with the dry ginger powder, green and black cardamoms, aniseed, cinnamon sticks, salt, garlic water, turmeric powder and pure ghee. Mix well and boil for 5-7 minutes.
4. Add the fried bottle gourd and the cooked yoghurt. Continue to cook until the bottle gourd is tender and the gravy thickens. Sprinkle the black cumin seeds and mix well.

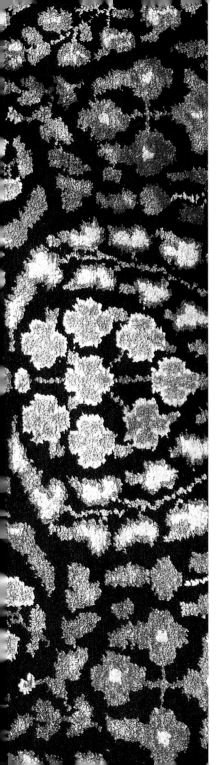

# Bom Chount

*Spicy apples in a tangy sauce*

### Ingredients

| | | | |
|---|---|---|---|
| 1 kg | apples (slightly sour to taste), peeled, cored, quartered | 125 gm | tamarind (*imli*), boiled in ½ cup water, strained |
| 10 cups / 2 lt | water | 2 tsp / 4 gm | Kashmiri red chilli powder, dissolved in ½ cup water |
| Salt to taste | | | |
| 8 | green cardamoms (*choti elaichi*) | ½ cup / 95 gm | pure (*desi*) ghee |
| 5 | cinnamon (*dalchini*) sticks, 1" each | ½ cup / 100 ml | dry cockscomb (*mawal*) flowers, heated with ¾ cup water, extract (see p. 17) |
| 4 tsp / 8 gm | turmeric (*haldi*) powder | | |
| ½ tsp / 1 gm | dry ginger powder (*sonth*) | ¼ tsp | black cumin seeds (*shah jeera*) |
| 1½ tbsp / 37 gm | onion paste, fried | | |

### Method

1. Fry the apples in refined oil until reddish brown. Remove with a slotted spoon and keep aside.
2. In a pan, bring the water mixed with salt to the boil on a high heat. Add the green cardamoms, cinnamon sticks, turmeric powder, dry ginger powder, onion paste and tamarind extract. Continue to boil the mixture until the liquid is reduced to half.
3. Add the fried apples, red chilli water and ghee. Cover the pan and cook the apples until they are tender and the pieces still retain their shape. Then add the cockscomb flower extract and boil for 2-3 minutes. Sprinkle the black cumin seeds. Mix well.

# Gogji

*Turnips flavoured with black cumin seeds*

## Ingredients

| | | | |
|---|---|---|---|
| 1 kg | turnips (*shalgam*), peeled, quartered and then rounded with a sharp knife | 1 tbsp / 25 gm | onion paste, fried |
| | | 2 tsp / 4 gm | Kashmiri red chilli powder, dissolved in ½ cup water |
| 10 cups / 2 lt | water | 1 tbsp / 15 ml | garlic (*lasan*) water (see p. 17) |
| 3 tsp / 6 gm | turmeric (*haldi*) powder | 1/3 cup / 65 gm | pure (*desi*) ghee |
| 5 | cinnamon (*dalchini*) sticks, 1" each | 1½ tbsp / 30 gm | sugar |
| | | ¼ cup / 50 ml | dry cockscomb (*mawal*) flowers, heated with 1 cup water, extract (see p. 17) |
| 8 | green cardamoms (choti elaichi) | | |
| 5 | black cardamoms (*bari elaichi*) | ¼ tsp | black cumin seeds (*shah jeera*) |
| Salt to taste | | | |

## Method

1. Mix 1 tsp salt with the turnips and keep them aside for 15 minutes. Wash and then fry them in refined oil until reddish brown in colour. Remove with a slotted spoon and keep aside.

2. In a deep pan, add the water, turmeric powder, cinnamon sticks, green and black cardamoms, salt, onion paste, red chilli water, garlic water and pure ghee. Bring the mixture to the boil, stirring continuously. Boil for 7-8 minutes.

3. Add the fried turnips and sugar. Cook till the turnips are tender. Add the cockscomb flower extract and the black cumin seeds. Mix well and simmer for 2-3 minutes.

# Choaq Vagan

*Spicy, red hot eggplant*

## Ingredients

| | | | |
|---|---|---|---|
| 1 kg | eggplant (*baingan*), small, peeled, with the stem intact | 2½ tsp / 5 gm | dry ginger powder (*sonth*) |
| | | 2 tbsp / 50 gm | onion paste, fried |
| 180 gm | tamarind (*imli*), boiled in 5 cups water, strained, extract | Salt to taste | |
| | | 3 tsp / 6 gm | Kashmiri red chilli powder, dissolved in 1 cup water |
| ½ cup / 100 ml | garlic (*lasan*) water (see p. 17) | | |
| 2 tsp / 4 gm | turmeric (*haldi*) powder | ⅓ cup / 57 ml | refined oil |
| 4 | cinnamon (*dalchini*) sticks, 2" each | 1 cup / 200 ml | dry cockscomb flowers (*mawal*), heated with 1 cup water, extract (see p. 17) |
| 6 | green cardamoms (*choti elaichi*) | | |
| 6 | black cardamoms (*bari elaichi*) | 1 tsp / 2 gm | black cumin seeds (*shah jeera*) |

## Method

1. Pierce the eggplants right across with a sharp knife. Then wash them in lightly salted water and fry them until reddish brown in colour. Drain and keep aside.
2. In a pan, add the tamarind extract, garlic water, turmeric powder, cinnamon sticks, green and black cardamoms, dry ginger powder, onion paste and salt. Bring the mixture to the boil. Add the red chilli water and 4 cups water. Bring the mixture to the boil again. Reduce the heat and add the refined oil. Cook until it is of a sauce-like consistency.
3. Add the fried eggplants, cockscomb flower extract and black cumin seeds. Simmer the mixture for another 10 minutes.

# Kan Gucchi

*Morel laced with yoghurt*

## Ingredients

| | | | |
|---|---|---|---|
| 100 gm | dried morel | 2 tsp / 4 gm | Kashmiri red chilli powder, |
| ½ cup / 85 ml | refined oil | | dissolved in ½ cup water |
| 4 | cinnamon (*dalchini*) sticks, | ½ tsp / 1 gm | dry ginger powder (*sonth*) |
| | 2" each | | Salt to taste |
| 8 | cloves (*laung*) | ⅓ cup / 66 ml | cooked yoghurt (see p. 17) |
| 8 | green cardamoms (*choti elaichi*) | 2 cups / 400 ml | water |
| | | 1 tbsp / 25 gm | onion paste, fried |
| 9 | black cardamoms (*bari elaichi*) | ¼ tsp | saffron (*zafran*) |
| | | ¼ tsp | black cumin seeds (*shah jeera*) |
| 1 tsp / 6 gm | garlic (*lasan*), paste | | |
| 1 tsp / 2 gm | turmeric (*haldi*) powder | ¼ tsp | dry mint (*pudina*) leaves |

## Method

1. Rehydrate the morels by putting them in water for 10-12 minutes. Drain and wash them in cold water. Remove the stems and slit them in two halves.
2. In a pan, add the morels, refined oil, cinnamon sticks, cloves, green and black cardamoms. Mix well and fry until all the water has dried up.
3. Add the garlic paste, turmeric powder, red chilli water, dry ginger powder and salt. Cook until the water has dried up completely.
4. Add the cooked yoghurt and stir until it is completely absorbed. Add the water, onion paste and saffron. Mix well. Reduce the heat to low and simmer for 10 minutes.
5. Sprinkle the black cumin seeds and dry mint leaves.

# Razmah

*Red kidney beans topped with butter*

## Ingredients

| | | | |
|---|---|---|---|
| 500 gm | red kidney beans (*rajmah*), soaked for 3 hours, washed, drained, | 3 tsp / 6 gm | turmeric (*haldi*) powder |
| 20 cups / 4 lt | water | 1½ tsp / 3 gm | dry ginger powder (*sonth*) |
| 7 | green cardamoms (*choti elaichi*) | Salt to taste | |
| | | 2 tbsp / 30 ml | garlic (*lasan*) water (see p. 17) |
| 5 | black cardamoms (*bari elaichi*) | 1½ tsp / 3 gm | Kashmiri red chilli powder, dissolved in 2 tbsp water |
| 4 | cinnamon (*dalchini*) sticks, 2" each | 2½ tbsp / 50 gm | butter |

## Method

1. In a deep pan, boil the red kidney beans with sufficient water. When soft, remove the pan from the heat and drain the liquid.
2. In the same pan, add the boiled kidney beans, water, green and black cardamoms, cinnamon sticks, turmeric powder, dry ginger powder, salt, garlic water and red chilli water. Bring the mixture to the boil. Cover and boil on low heat until the beans are tender and semi-dry. Add more water, if required.
3. Top with butter. Serve hot with steamed rice.

# Kashmiri Palow

*Fragrant Kashmiri rice*

### Ingredients

| | | | |
|---|---|---|---|
| 3 cups | Basmati rice, washed | | (*dalchini*) sticks, 2" each |
| **For the stock:** | | Salt to taste | |
| 15 cups / 3 lt | water | 1½ cups / 360 gm | onions, sliced, fried until brown, drained |
| 6 | large bones from the leg of lamb | | |
| 5 | bay leaves (*tej patta*) | ¾ tbsp / 8 gm | black cumin seeds (*shah jeera*) |
| 15 | black cardamoms (*bari elaichi*) | 8 | green cardamoms (*choti elaichi*) |
| 2½ tbsp / 10 gm | fennel (*saunf*) seeds | ½ cup / 95 gm | pure (*desi*) ghee |
| 4 | cinnamon | | |

### Method

1. **For the stock,** bring all the ingredients (except the onion) to the boil in a deep pan. Cover and continue to boil for 15-18 minutes. Now add the browned onions and boil for another 5 minutes. Remove from heat and keep aside to cool. Strain the stock through a muslin cloth to get 7 cups stock. Add more water, if required. Keep aside. Discard the bones and whole spices.
2. Bring the strained stock to the boil in a deep pan, add the rice, black cumin seeds and green cardamoms. Bring the mixture to the boil, then reduce the heat and cook until the rice is ¾ done.
3. Heat the ghee in another pan; when hot, pour in the rice mixture.
4. Cover the pan with a tight lid and cook on very low heat until the rice is cooked just right.

# Zirish Chetin

*Zirish chutney*

## Ingredients

| | | | |
|---|---|---|---|
| 50 gm | *zirish*, washed, soaked for 15 minutes, made into a paste. | 1 tsp / 2 gm | Kashmiri red chilli powder |
| 4 tbsp / 25 gm | tamarind (*imli*), boiled with ¼ cup water, strained | ¼ tsp | black pepper (*kali mirch*) powder |
| | | Salt to taste | |

## Method

1. Mix all the ingredients together to a fine paste.

# Gand Chetin

*Onion chutney*

## Ingredients

| | | | |
|---|---|---|---|
| 2 cups / 500 gm | onion, sliced | ½ tsp / 1 gm | black cumin seeds (*shah jeera*) |
| ½ cup | green chillies, deseeded, chopped | ½ tsp | dry mint (*pudina*) leaves |
| ½ cup / 12½ gm | green coriander (*hara dhaniya*), chopped | 2 tsp / 4 gm | Kashmiri red chilli powder |
| | | 1 cup / 200 ml | vinegar (*sirka*) |
| | | Salt to taste | |

## Method

1. Mix 1 tbsp salt with the onions. Keep aside for a minute. Then wash the onions and drain the water completely.
2. In a bowl, mix all the ingredients together and cool in a refrigerator.

# Dodh Al

*Pumpkin relish*

## Ingredients

| | | | |
|---|---|---|---|
| 350 gm | pumpkin (*kaddu*), peeled, deseeded, cut into large pieces | 1¾ tbsp / 20 ml | honey |
| 4 cups / 800 ml | water | ½ tsp / 2 gm | salt |
| 10 cloves | garlic (*lasan*) | ¼ tsp | black cumin seeds (*shah jeera*) |
| 1 cup / 180 gm | yoghurt (*dahi*), hung | ¼ tsp | saffron (*zafran*) ground |
| | | 1½ tbsp / 15 gm | raisins (*kishmish*) |

## Method

1. In a deep-bottomed pan, boil the pumpkin with water and garlic until it is tender. Remove the pan from the heat, drain water, and cool. Remove and discard the garlic cloves and then mash the pumpkin. Put it in a muslin cloth and squeeze out as much of water as possible.
2. Transfer the mashed pumpkin into a bowl, add the remaining ingredients, and mix well.

# Doon Chetin

*Walnut chutney*

## Ingredients

| | | | |
|---|---|---|---|
| 50 gm | walnut (*akhrot*) kernels, washed, ground coarsely | Salt to taste | |
| 1 tbsp | onion | 1 tsp | green coriander (*hara dhaniya*), chopped |
| ¼ cup | green chillies | 1 cup / 180 gm | yoghurt (*dahi*), hung in a muslin cloth for 2 hours |
| ¼ tsp | black cumin seeds (*shah jeera*) | | |
| ¼ tsp | dry mint (*pudina*) leaves | | |

## Method

1. Mince the onion and green chillies together and mix all the ingredients together.

# Kong Firin

*Saffron-flavoured semolina garnished with dry fruits*

## Ingredients

| | | | |
|---|---|---|---|
| + cups / 720 ml | full-cream milk | ½ cup / 110 gm | sweetened |
| ¼ tsp | saffron (*zafran*) | | condensed milk |
| + tbsp / 40 gm | semolina (*suji*), | ½ tsp | vetiver (*kewda*) |
| | washed | | essence |
| ⅓ cup / 50 gm | sugar | 1½ tbsp / 22 gm | cashew nuts |
| 1 cup / 100 gm | wholemilk fudge | | (*kaju*), chopped |
| | (*khoya*) **or** | 1½ tbsp | pistachios (*pista*) |

## Method

1. Boil the full cream milk and saffron together, stirring all the time, for 3-4 minutes.
2. To the boiling milk, add the semolina and stir continuously, until the milk thickens to a sauce-like consistency.
3. Add the sugar, wholemilk fudge or sweetened condensed milk and vetiver essence, and cook it for a further 2-3 minutes.
4. Cool and pour into small serving bowls and garnish with cashew nuts and pistachios. Keep in the refrigerator to set.

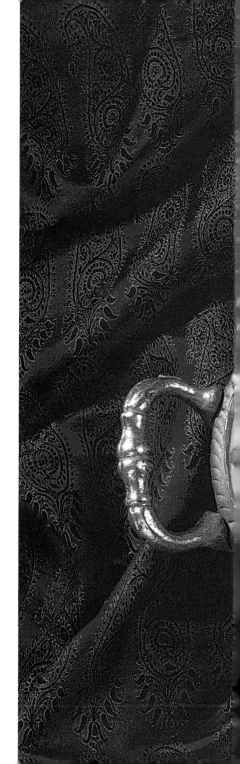

# Halwa

*Semolina pudding with dry fruits*

## Ingredients

| | | | |
|---|---|---|---|
| 2½ cups / 250 gm | semolina (*suji*), fine quality | ¼ cup / 60 gm | coconut (*nariyal*), grated |
| 8 cups / 1600 ml | water | 2 cups / 300 gm | sugar |
| 1½ tsp / 1½ gm | saffron (*zafran*), ground | 1 tbsp / 10 gm | raisins (*kishmish*) |
| 1½ cups / 285 gm | pure (*desi*) ghee | 2 tbsp / 8 gm | coconut (*nariyal*), grated |
| ½ cup / 50 gm | raisins (*kishmish*) | 2 tbsp / 30 gm | cashew nuts (*kaju*) |

## Method

1. Boil the water with the saffron. Simmer for 15 minutes.
2. In another pan, heat the ghee; add the semolina and fry until reddish brown in colour.
3. Add the saffron water and mix thoroughly. Add the raisins, coconut and sugar. Keep stirring until it is mixed well and is of a thick sauce-like consistency.
4. Garnish with raisins, coconut and cashew nuts.

# Index